AMERICAN HOLIDAYS

VETERANS DAY

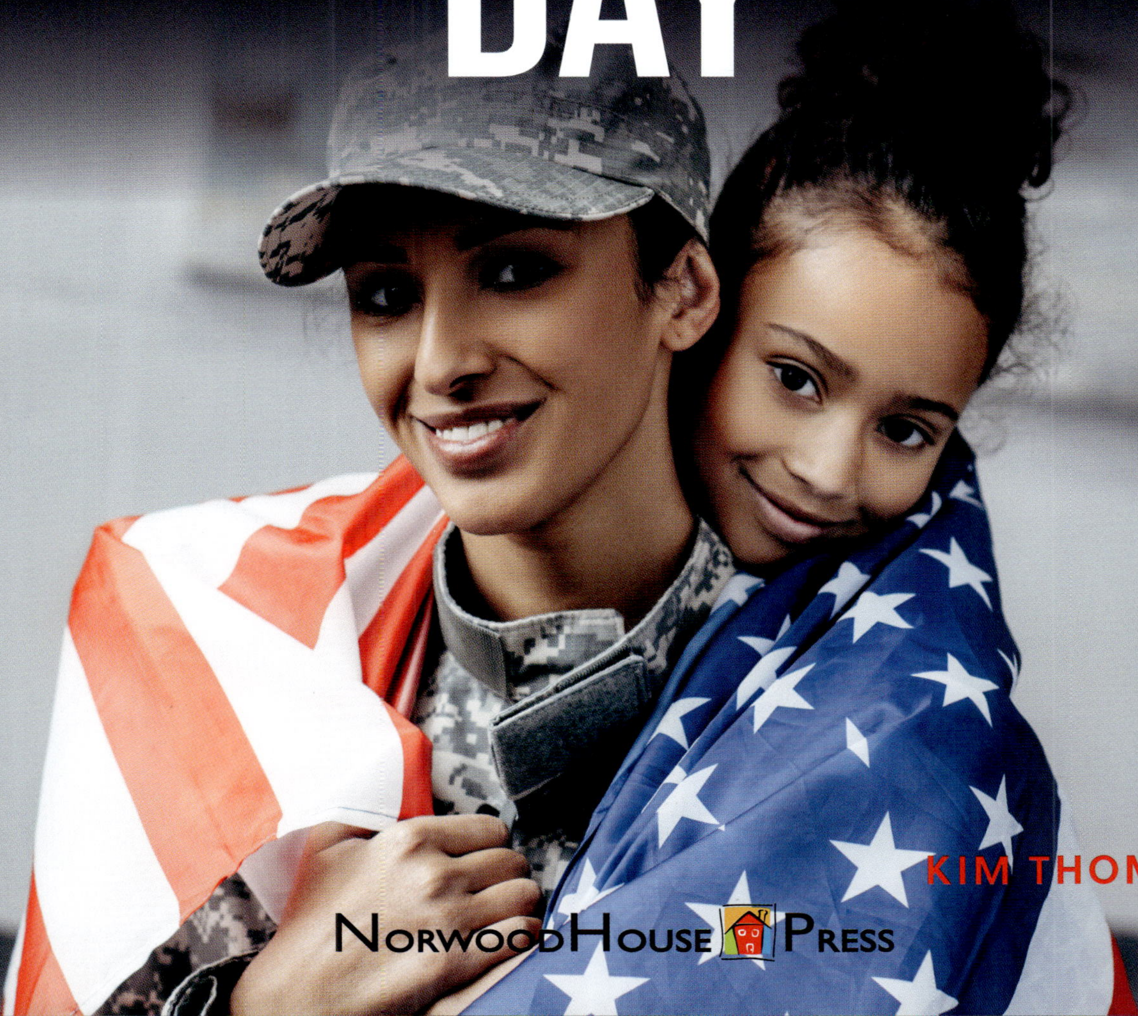

KIM THOMPSON

NORWOOD HOUSE PRESS

Cataloging-in-Publication Data

Names: Thompson, Kim.
Title: Veterans Day / Kim Thompson.
Description: Buffalo, NY : Norwood House Press, 2026. | Series: American holidays | Includes glossary and index.
Identifiers: ISBN 9781978575288 (pbk.) | ISBN 9781978575295 (library bound) | ISBN 9781978575301 (ebook)
Subjects: LCSH: Veterans Day--Juvenile literature.
Classification: LCC D671.T466 2026 | DDC 394.264--dc23

Published in 2026 by
Norwood House Press
2544 Clinton Street
Buffalo, NY 14224

Designer: Rhea Magaro

Photo credits: Cover, p.1 LightField Studios/Shutterstock.com; p. 4 Everett Collection; pp. 5, 6 Library of Congress; p. 9 OogImages/Shutterstock.com; p. 11 SeventyFour/Shutterstock.com; pp. 12, 13 U.S. Department of Defense ;p. 14 karen roach/Shutterstock.com; p. 15 Derek PolenaKatsaros/Shutterstock.com; p. 17 PixelShot/Shutterstock.com; p. 18 MSgt Kristin duBois/Shutterstock.com; p. 19 Mie Ahmt/Shutterstock.com; p. 21 Evgeniy Kalinovskiy/Shutterstock.com;

Printed in the United States of America

CPSIA compliance information: Batch #CSNHP26: For further information contact Norwood House Press at 1-800-237-9932.

TABLE OF CONTENTS

HOW IT BEGAN

In 1918, the fighting in World War I was over. America had helped win the war. Peace began on November 11th at 11:00 a.m. It was the 11th hour on the 11th day of the 11th month of the year.

Americans began to celebrate each year on November 11th. People held parades. At 11:00, everyone paused to remember the soldiers who fought in the war. The holiday was called **Armistice** Day.

By 1945, U.S. soldiers had helped win World War II. People wanted a holiday to honor all the nation's **veterans**. In 1954, Armistice Day was renamed Veterans Day.

Veterans Day is on November 11th, no matter which day of the week the date falls on. It honors all people who have served in the military during times of war or peace.

Each year, the U.S. President gives a Veterans Day **Proclamation**. In 2023, President Joseph Biden said, "This Veterans Day, we honor the generations of women and men who have served and **sacrificed**—not for a person, a place, or a President—but for an idea unlike any other: the idea of the United States of America. For nearly 250 years, our veterans have defended the **values** that make us strong so that our Nation could stand as a **citadel** of **liberty**."

OF THE PRESIDENT OF THE UNITED

FOR THE LIVING

America has another holiday, Memorial Day, for remembering soldiers who died in battle. Veterans Day is different. It recognizes living people who once served in the military or who are serving now. This might include your neighbors and family members.

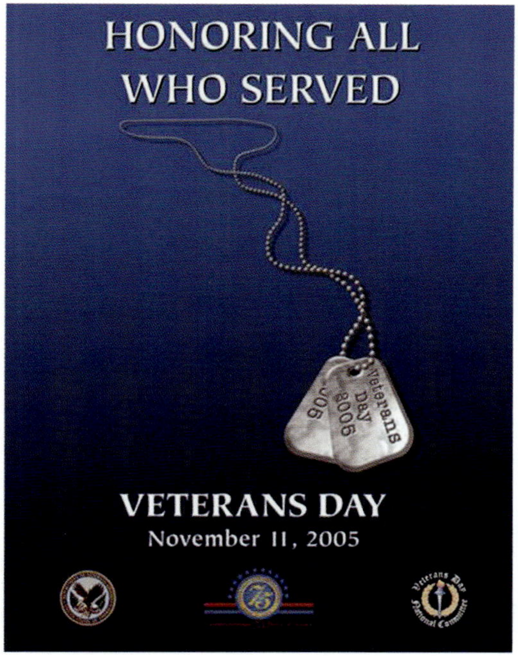
HONORING ALL WHO SERVED
Veterans Day 2006
VETERANS DAY
November 11, 2005

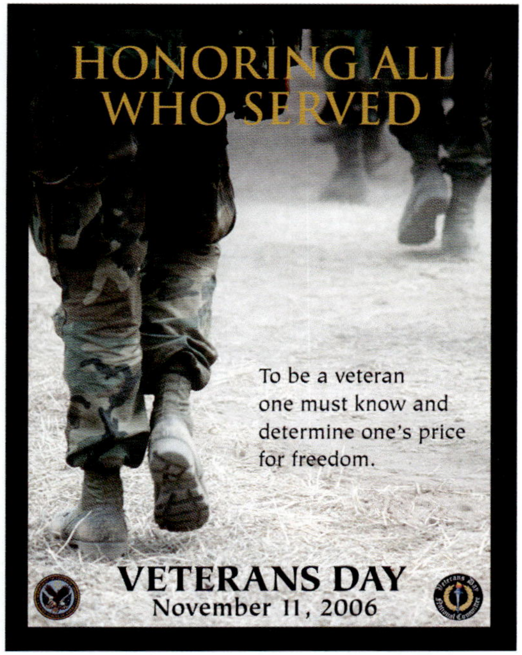
HONORING ALL WHO SERVED
To be a veteran one must know and determine one's price for freedom.
VETERANS DAY
November 11, 2006

HONORING ALL WHO SERVED
VETERANS DAY
NOVEMBER 11, 2007

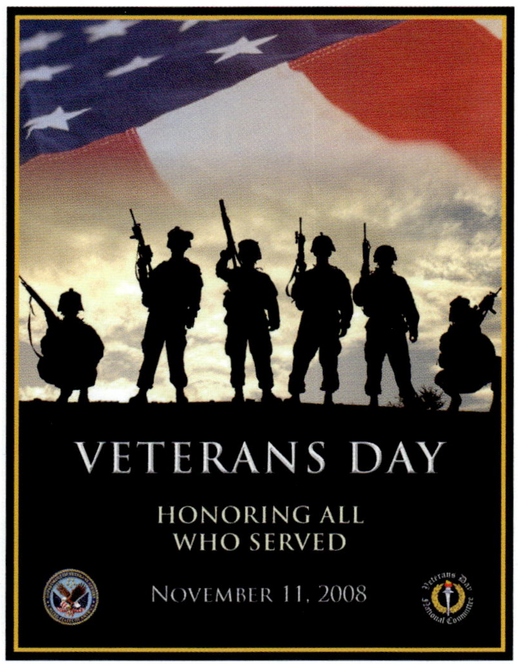
VETERANS DAY
HONORING ALL WHO SERVED
NOVEMBER 11, 2008

Veterans Day celebrates people from all branches of the armed forces: the U.S. Army, Marine Corps, Navy, Air Force, Space Force, and Coast Guard. Each year, the Veterans Day National Committee creates a special poster to honor them.

A NATIONAL HOLIDAY

On Veterans Day, government offices are closed. Some schools and businesses close too.

Towns hold parades to recognize veterans. There are special assemblies, flag raising ceremonies, and church services. People say "The Pledge of Allegiance." They sing **patriotic** songs.

Veterans and **active duty** military get into parks and museums free. Some restaurants give them free coffee and meals. Many Americans find special ways to say “thank you” to veterans.

A Veterans Day ceremony is held at Arlington National Cemetery in Arlington, Virginia. The U.S. President often lays a wreath on the Tomb of the Unknown Soldier.

Each year, Americans observe two minutes of silence to honor veterans. This moment of silence begins at 11:11 a.m. on the West Coast or 2:11 p.m. on the East Coast.

THANK YOU, VETERANS!

On Veterans Day, America celebrates all past and present members of the military. The nation thanks them for their service and sacrifice. People show **respect** to those willing to fight to make the country strong and free.

GLOSSARY

active duty (AK-tiv DOO-tee): employed as a current, full-time member of the military

armistice (AHR-muh-stuhs): an agreement to stop fighting during a war

citadel (SIT-uh-del): a fortress or castle that overlooks and protects a city

liberty (LIB-ur-tee): freedom

patriotic (pay-tree-AH-tik): full of loyalty and love for your country

proclamation (prah-kluh-MAY-shuhn): a public announcement

respect (ri-SPEKT): a feeling of admiration and appreciation

sacrificed (SAK-ruh-fised): gave up something you value, such as your time, for the sake of something that is more important

values (VAL-yooz): things you believe in; things that are precious or important to you

veterans (VET-ur-uhnz): people who have served in the armed forces, especially during a war

THINKING QUESTIONS

1. What was Armistice Day?
2. What happened between 1918 and 1945?
3. What is the difference between Veterans Day and Memorial Day?
4. What special events happen on Veterans Day?
5. Name the branches of the United States military.

INDEX

ABOUT THE AUTHOR

Kim Thompson is a teacher and writer from Columbus, Ohio. Her grandfathers served during World War II. Her father fought in the Vietnam War. Kim is grateful for their service and for all military members who have made sacrifices for our country.